She Didn't Mean to Do It

1999 *Agnes Lynch Starrett Poetry Prize*

PITT POETRY SERIES

Ed Ochester, Editor

She Didn't Mean to Do It

Daisy Fried

University of Pittsburgh Press

The publication of this book is supported by a grant from the Pennsylvania Council on the Arts.

Published by the University of Pittsburgh Press, Pittsburgh, Pa. 15261

For Jim Quinn,

who knows everything and denies it

Contents

I

2000	3
Carnival in Spring	4
Then Comes the Girl with the Tampon in Her	5
A Story Having to Do with Walt Whitman	7
Whatever Works	9
57 May Women Near Our Lady of Ransom	10
She Didn't Mean to Do It	15
Electric Slide	16

II

Little Girls Weaving	21
Settled	22
Correggio	23
Slaughterhouse Island	24
Fishtown Song	28
Romance Novel	29
Bulrush	30
Bollocks by the Thames	31
Ice	33
Water	34
Steam	35
Moving Her Around	36
The Kites	38
Trooper	39
Wit's End	41

III

Azalea Garden   45

The Means   46

Duet for a Button Store: lyrics without music   47

Only Envy   50

One in the Hand   51

Him Again   53

Princess Counting Peas   54

The Bombing of Serbia

      I. The Beauty of Boys on Skateboards   55

      II. River   56

Clean   57

Strike   58

Acknowledgments   71

I

New Year's Eve, it's 6 p.m. Bar door
on the corner opens and closes, it's just
silver slipping and slamming but first
a run of heat through the door, the shine
in the black of spigots and mirrors
and bottles and desire without method
and two men on some stools, womanless, elbows
slid together, cardboard hats reading *"ewYea"*
in glitter that rains down and the door
shuts. Puddles by the curb, a little jazz
of rain. A girl down there showing her teeth
to a man, her voice all made of sirens
and rocks and dirty butter and cheap stockings,
preg again or out of dope or don't hit me
or don't leave me or what will I do
or take me with you and silence. Where the
wind goes when there is no wind. What
you will never be because you don't know
how to want to. If you cannot take me
under cover of night, if you cannot save
the whole world, what will become of me?

Carnival in Spring

Stabbed, the girl, sixteen, fell back into her girl-
friends' hands, spoke: *Guys, I can't breathe,* and so, she died.
Who's crying in the lights of the carnival

tonight? The stabber, a girl, also sixteen,
forgot the swinging of the Ferris wheel seats,
the shitty roller coaster, the boy she came to see.
Once pushed, her hair fell down, she stabbed her,
and ran away, and was taken away.
Who's crying at the carnival in the lights

tonight? I saw that the wisteria
in dusk its same color hung (heavier than
the breasts of stabbed and stabber ever would be)
overgrown by leaves, and so, summer. *Who's*

crying? Watch it and you'll not say where's the time
gone. You'll know, you'll see it go, it's gone. *Go, oh,
who?* The girl fell back, died before the roses
were fully bloomed, after the magnolias

died. Died somewhat like a magnolia dies
and lives: sloppy petals spreading, now slipping,
and stopping now, now falling. In a year the carnival
will come again. It does. Like buds.

It does. A thing to watch, a thing to mark, wait,
whisper. *Don't cry at the carnival in the
brightened tonight. Oh pity, oh pity guys.*
Guys, I cannot breathe, I cannot see the night.

Then Comes the Girl with the Tampon in Her

Lights out, shades down, boys out,
projector on, ticky whir, light-lit
dust planets hang in horizontal
search-beam cone. Mean girl, queen girl,
dork girl, embarrassed girl, hated girl:
we all sit quiet, intent: it's fifth grade
menstruation movie: man (man!) narrator
describes the shape of things to come:
fiddle-headed ovaries, those fluctuant fists
on cartoon stems; long short monthly
journey of first egg out from either
side; the flux, the slough, the cycle of days,
months, moons, myths, xx and xy even.
All this of course we knew already.

Then comes the girl with the tampon in her,
high on the high board over a shining pool,
gleaming white tank suit, pale hair
wet and straight, face brave, and we know
she can do anything. Steps, one two three,
across the screen, skips, bounces, pushes
herself up and out, arms victoried, kiltered
in air, white in white sky, white in her,
then swoop, into water, so white
she dissolves under, into our memories.

Mean girl, queen girl, dork girl,
all girls concentrate as one in livid
public school dark. Teacher, usually
pissed off and fussy, sits in back nodding,
weirdly convivial, motherly, chummy. Down

the hall, an empty bathroom, with drippy taps
and theoretical fucks and cocks, with girls'
best-loved boys' names written up. Twenty years
later, grown up, apart, each, helpless not
to remember the white-suited girl, tampon built
clothy always and clean, unred, unlogged,
unleakable, into the soft inside her pelvis,
surfaces to breathe, swims to side,
clambers out, climbs, strides, dives
again, over and over, telling us that
we knew, that we are, diving through
us, what we would always have to be.

A Story Having to Do with Walt Whitman

A friend of mine used to be, and still is, but only
legally, married to a dancer. The girl, this dancer,
his wife, had a teacher, one of those beautiful menschy
dancer men, who was dying of AIDS. He, the teacher,
as I imagine it, though it's not always true for dancers
in his company, had done nothing in his life but dance.
Well, that's perfectly enough. But the girl, this dancer, this
wife, who read as well as danced, thought she would bring him
Leaves of Grass, with the not inconsiderable presumption
that it would comfort him to the great end. (Presumptions need
not be false. It would have.) But this girl, the dancer, the wife,
once she realized that she had presumed, ascribing to her
gift and thus to herself a certain importance, worried
about it so much that she put off bringing it to him.

He lay at home and sometimes in the hospital, with
many friends in bright-colored clothes around him (they all used
to wear black and white, but thinking of death, they put on
rainbows). The girl, the wife, the dancer, worried and worried
about walking into the room of many colors. It
was not her wardrobe, she was not worried about that, though
she wore mostly grays, maroons, browns. She worried about
stepping forward in that crowd, having them look at her,
who did not even know if the dying man cared about her.
She worried she would be seen for what she was, not a friend,
but a pupil, and adorer. So he died and she
never brought the book. When she realized her foolishness,
as she always did, immediately after the moment
when it was too late, she just went down to the East River

and sat on a pier and looked at Manhattan and felt shame.
The book, a pretty hardback, in her lap. She sat and read

it, the whole thing. She thought several things as she read. One,
how can you die, not having read everything. Another,
how all actions should be as if for others, even if
none truly are. Three, how awful to die in the summer.
Four. She missed her husband, my friend. Five. She must work harder
at dancing. Six, what did it really matter if he
never read Leaves of Grass. Did it matter to the soul?
Seven, oh for goodness sake, what soul? The next day, she
agreed at his funeral to help clean out his
apartment. On his coffee table there was a Monet
with bad reproductions, Richardson's Life of Picasso,
Vol. 2 (the cubist years), autobiographies of

choreographers, and a battered paperback: Leaves of
Grass, what do you think? She opened it and found it all marked
up inside, with comments and all. Comments about how one could
make a dance with all this in mind. And she all of a
sudden remembered seeing the title "Afraid of the
Merge" on his list of choreography credits. Inside
the front cover it said "To my darling, from Gary." Instead
of this making this girl, the dancer, the wife laugh, or see the
humor in the whole thing, or at least see that she had read
him right, and picked the right gift, she just felt miserable.
This is why my friend and she had trouble getting along, for
he is not so complex and constipated as this girl, this
dancer, his wife. What happened? Oh, I expect she'll get over
it. Oh, one more thing. I am the girl, this dancer, this wife.

Whatever Works

"I never was much good at blow jobs," she says, driving.
"Couldn't get the right amount of pressure. Or maybe
it was him. He just didn't like them. He said so:
'maybe it's me,' he said. After awhile I just
stopped worrying about it, and here we are." I'm
sitting in the back to keep an eye on her baby.
I nod, thinking what I know, what I don't know. Old
music. Turn off that old radio music. The
baby's crying. More night inside the car than out.
The baby's crying despite she pulled over at
the rest stop to feed it just ten, twenty miles back. I keep on
pushing its rubber nipple at its mouth; it takes
it a moment then goes on crying. Finally,
entering the bridge, she reaches her arm back over the seat,
finds the baby's mouth with her finger. It
knows her skin by taste. Mouths that finger, sucks it,
chews it, falls asleep. "Whatever works," she says,
and keeps on driving fast and crooked around that way.

In May, female locust trees bloom—
    pale sex flower, honey scent—
males on my adopted block dangle only green,
    green leaves—
girls, in four May movements, make the parish ripple
    with celebration,
weekend following weekend under the queeny locusts.

I. 50 First Communions

Six-piece fifth-grade cornet band blasting,
Sunday mid-day. Baby brides line up in rows,
fingers pressed under chins in imitation
of prayer, hair curled over ears, or strung
through bead tiaras, or speckled with fabric flowers.
Bodies spazzy with childhood, they jig in unraveling
lines at the parish schoolyard gate. Buckle shoes
creak and blister feet, lacy tights itch, creep
down legs under princess-waist dresses—white as
shirts of boys who'll paw them ten years on—
that billow when they spin. They stand on tiptoe,
dance trying not to pee themselves, chew
fingertips, suck thumbs—there's Carmela
from two doors down—who steals pansies from
my windowboxes—I pretend I don't know—
she makes them multiply. Folding net wings
over her shoulders, she compares her Bride of Jesus
ring to other girls' identical ones. Sudden
tuneless cornet blast—two-way traffic stops

in the street. The little girls jaywalk between fenders;
moms wave, dads videocam, grandmas cry *bella!*
and kiss their fingertips. I go back to pinching
dead heads off my pansies as 50 girls disappear
up church steps for the first swallowing, in the first
last long everlasting hour of ballerina belief.

II. One First Morning After

Idling engine, just dawn. Exhaust stink enters
my room from out there. Cardoor thunk. Cough,
stumble, skirt rip—"shit!" (suffocated)—boy's voice:
"bye babe": next-door-Kelly, 16, returning prom queen,
makes the street's only early sounds. Most times
haughtily kind in her teenage beauty, she limps up
her stoop, no-longer-drunk Cinderella home
from the ball, changed, and the same, and changed.
Street lamps flick out. Four years so far
since I moved here, girls come home like this
just before the sun, sometimes from the mountains,
sometimes the shore—"we're going down
Wildwood after," Kelly told me when she
showed me her dress yesterday. I see it like a movie:
late slowdances, pale blue bodice pressed
to his fierce cummerbund, she thinks "does he?
do I? does my?" She and her pals ride
groped, groping, away from the festooned
hotel. At land's edge, sling-back sandals hung on
two fingers, she runs, pantyhose streaming off
her other hand like a standard, till she flings them
somewhere into the wind. Gathers scrunch of gown
into her fist, dips her bare toes, so as to shriek,

jump back, be hugged, not be let go, till deciding,
she goes to the neon motel—where she crouches in front of
her gasping astonished boy—maneuvers
her limbs with him through studied juttings—watches
ceiling fan turn slowly, watches still mirror, watches
heap of iridescent dress on nearby chair quiver—
watches herself rock, thinking "so this is, so this
is fucking."
                     Home in lapsing night. Inside
her door, church's first chiming driving through her,
she trembles, enervated, unnerved, in the locust
dawn, knowing unknowing something
she's passed through

> neighbor ladies waking tilt their blinds to see and tsk
> but maybe like me remember their own May beds,
> not so young as Kelly, but young, and the bed made,
> I and another on top of it, the sun slanting, an oak tree
> pressing against the windowscreen, that body never
> loved before or since pressing mine,
> and the next day, still May, I went and sat
> on a big rock awhile

             thinking so this is—done, finally, done.

III. Four Last Nights Before

Screaming's the first you hear of them, like crazed
laughing of gulls who slide over our rowhouses
from the river some blocks east. Then you turn, you see
who screes: four bachelorettes, at watching, embarrassed men.
Limo white as communion dresses has picked up Teresa

from around the corner, who always yells "hi, lovebirds!"
when I pass by with my boyfriend, and moves her car
when I can't fit my own in. Stalled
in Saturday night party-strip traffic—carsfull
of kids cruising, honking, shaken by thumping
big-watt sound systems—others wading up and down
the sidewalk, swiveling heads at promising flesh—
Teresa and friends (no diff, bride from bridesmaids
this night) squeeze breast to breast standing through
the limo roofhole, bighaired mermaids waving
weaving arms, mythic fish halves hidden below
behind blacked-out windows. The limo jolts—
someone's sparkly purse falls down the side
of the car, spills compacts, tampons like shotgun shells,
plastic wand for birth control foam, pens,
pills—scree! another jolt, whoops!—nippleflash,
scree, scree!—cop directing traffic
smiles, adjusts his belt; he bends unembarrassed,
collects wand, Delfen foam canister, o.b.'s and all,
crams them back into the pocketbook, hands it up
to Teresa, who smirks, takes out eye pencil, blue
or black, plus a scrap of paper, scribbles something
against her hand—phone number?—wads it,
tosses it down to him, blue-purple nails lustrous
in crisscrossing headlights. Eeee, Tereese!

        The long car moves on,
the bachelorettes—harpies, seals barking, sirens
singing the song of themselves, readying
one of their kind for the long dive—oh, bachelorettes scree:
come, here, yo stud, yo, come on, hey yo—

           for tomorrow we lose her.

IV. Our L of R, May morn, on a line from Pablo Neruda

The janitor cleans Mary.
Sings to her as he scrubs her breasts
and the steps so that
under brides' feet
they shine.

Time, girls, time.

She Didn't Mean to Do It

Oh, she was sad, oh, she was sad.
She didn't mean to do it.

Certain thrills stay tucked in your limbs,
go no further than your fingers, move your legs through their paces,
but no more. Certain thrills knock you flat
on your sheets on your bed in your room and you fade
and they fade. You falter and they're gone, gone, gone.
Certain thrills puff off you like smoke rings,
some like bell rings growing out, out, turning
brass, steel, gold, till the whole world's filled
with the gonging of your thrills.

But oh, she was sad, she was just sad, sad,
and she didn't mean to do it.

The pregnant girls break me in. *Don't be freaked. There's only*
    one bathroom. Push, bang,
they open the door: *GIRLS IN!* they shout. Men come out—
    gentlemen. We're in,
and *wow,* I say. Mirrors, sinks, broke down urinals with their little
    yellow pools of piss
like lemon syrup in china teacups. But everything else, cunt. Glaring
    maws. Rows rising.
Tacked up. Taped up. Full-color. Oh, the legs of the pinup girls,
    they're shiny, smoothed
as bronze saints' feet that've been touched and kissed and kissed
    for centuries, and oh,
stars, moons, sheaves and the brambles that veins, hairs, moles
    and other marks make
on skin, all that's brushed to nothing, poreless eggshell, silicone lips,
    plasticene hillocks of ass.
Backdrop to the main event. Unbrushed. Real. Gasping
    gaping undergrowth,
hairy, staring, brackish, slack, gleam, bluster, glister, blast, bloat,

    blossom, blow. . .
Stop. We're in the basement, under Bloomingdale's.
    The pregnant girls
are 17, 19; me, younger, at 23. Dark here, smell of mildew,
    male sweat, washrag,
sick bouquet that follows a fart. Mangle of mops, pushbrooms,
    tarp rolls, bales of wire,
tools, screws, nails, fuses. The pregnant girls break me in,
    show me easy,
what to do: take fix-up orders from the store upstairs, pass them
    to the repairmen

who walk out of the dark. *S'up ladies.* They really are gentlemen.
       We have no bathroom.
It's theirs we use. The pregnant girls prop their bellies
       on the sinks,
orange-stick their nails, do their lips in the redsy colors
       they say they
look best in; blasé, amused, laugh at me looking
       (grizzly, shoved up cunts).

So I take a felt pen—*no!* they scream. So I light a cigarette,
       they look at it longing—
Girl One sucks a cinnamon stick (wiry tufts, runnels of hair)
       Girl Two mouths her
charm necklace (cunts in color, the details so loving). They lick
       their lips to wipe
away wanting, turn away, wash hands, complain. Girl One, gold
    earrings
       banging her cheeks:
My back, my legs, eyes, tongue, teeth, tits. Hand holding her back low down.
       My gas pains, these breasts,
these damn breasts already leaking milk. Girl Two tilts, spits, spits out
       charms: *my bladder*—
Oh girl, my bladder, I counted I peed like 26 times last night—
       Well last time
I kneeled in church it took two strong men to haul me up again. They turn up
       their shirts to show
stretchmarks that root through drumtight skin; through sheer panty
    hose,
       show veintrees that firework
their young-girl calves. And we've got the radio on, its tinny sound,

       its busted antenna.
And "Electric Slide" comes on; they both cry up in delight, begin to
    dance.

I don't know how
but they pull me in, and we're step, tilt, turn, clap, hip going that way,
shoulders the other—
BamBamBam—Ladies? hey? you coming out ever? Men massed outside.
Ungently waiting. *Bam!*
I stop dancing, about to leave, but the pregnant girls run at the door,
block and double-lock it,
BOYS OUT! They turn up the music, make me dance between them,
teaching me their job.
Swing bellies past sinks, urinals, the watchful hairy blind rise of
Cyclop
cunts. I crash
into the weight of their children. It sets me in the right direction.
They fill up cold space
with their squat bodies. I learn it, I know it. My dry and normal
and future body,
dancing easy now, dancing for them.

II

Little Girls Weaving

*On the road from the Turkish town of Selcuk to the archaeological site of Ephesus there
is a factory where tourists can buy rugs and watch them being made.*

There are little girls weaving when you walk out in the morning,
and little girls weaving when you walk back at night. In weaving,
the hands, which have a thousand angles—bird, mallet, poultice,
    purse,
signal, letter, clay wad, smoke—are merely pushed by the arms;
the arms are hung upon the back. Sense of balance is required. Little
    girls have that.

In the museum, Cybele stands up with her trophy testicles.
Priapus stands up with his giant cock's burden of fruit. I
believe in this world of heroes. Little girls weaving don't stand up.
Little girls weaving make no sound. You've got to imagine
the gathering sighing sounds. *Ehrr, huhh, ussh.* Small sounds,
kept inside the shell of the skin, inside little girl lungs. Pushed by the
    arms,
arms hung on the back. Sense of balance is required. Little girls have
    that.

Settled

After they filled in the tributary streams with factory ash
    in 1919, there was no more
going to town by boat by river on fine days: suddenly you
    simply walked or rode across
what was, before, marsh, marshwater. They say it changed your
    thought of yourself or your place:
you didn't go to town, now you were town. And they built houses
    on those new beds, but then
the ash began to wash out, the houses to sink. It's in the porch
    first, the unsupported sag
of the porch roof; next, cracks, in the plaster walls; a marble
    put carefully on a rugless floor
rolls on its own till it hits wall; then standing out front,
    shaking your head, you see
the whole battered thing sinking, sinking and settling, a tired
    man who has worked all his life
sinking to his couch, one hip, shoulder down with it, other hip,
    shoulder down with it,
face deflecting an unsayable ache, a tired man who has worked
    monstrously all his life
taking and following orders, no choice, no choice but to do it
    well—perhaps no thought
to do it otherwise—and do it again, tomorrow and more tomorrow—
    well eventually
the family goes, the whole thing collapses, and a long time after,
    no one remembers, or wants to.

Correggio

There are things I want so badly
    and then I don't want them at all,
so I go to sleep and when I wake up
    it's not desire in heart, crotch, lungs

or brain, it's outside myself and coming
    at me like the Smog Monster
or that thumb of mossy Jove-smoke
    that climbs around Io, nudging

under her arm and around her back,
    slowly jibbing her backward off
her stump. It's not how her head is slipped
    in its socket on the top end

of her neck. It's how the one hand
    drops to bring the smog-thing closer;
how the pale other flutters up like a sea-
    weed wad, boneless, glad to the dark.

Slaughterhouse Island

Dumb luck. The bad kids play nasty with a rat.
Shot it. Here the canal begins and the river
turns from it. Bad kids,
they swing the rat sort of at me.
Pissing the night away I run by on the towpath;
no headphones but the pop song line
I heard this morning sticks in my head. *PISS, NIGHT* and *WAY*
come out hard with each right leg stride.
Snow geese string the sky high up in necklace strands,
white blinking constellations, shift and wing at the sun.

Such sun. I ignore the kids
or wave back, I forget, and panting,
then breath smoothing out, I reach path's end,
turn back. I hear the pop pop of target pistols
of the bad kids hunting the rats for sport,
rats that ran out as if in surrender
from the shut abattoir when the shovels came in.
Steamshovels, backhoes, bulldozers, booms, massed
on the island to tear the slaughterhouse down—jump
their yellow bodies at the walls, bite out chunks,
score the walls till only crumbs of stone still
swing slightly, caught
on stubborn infrastructure wire web,
and ashy dust puffs through new gaps—
yet to begin. My grandmother

worked there from 14. Sat out on the berm,
yo, years ago, where the bad kids are rampaging,

to eat her lunches with the other slaughterhouse kids.
All of them trying to find a husband or wife
in the half hour per day they had of the sun.
For they arrived before light, for they
went home in the dark. No geese here then.
Dumb luck, or something else, she found
my grandfather, a man strong enough
for her to stick to, and she did,
like memory strangely sticks, like wise tragic
grandmas stick around poems, bah. Bah!

℥

Bah. Bad nasty kids, girls and boys
I recognize from my block
careen and crash through cattails,
purple loosestrife blaze, other tasseled rushes. Boys and girls
squat like cops on *New York Undercover*,
glare, two-hand their pistols,
gone wacko, shoot trees, shoot rats, shoot rocks.
Shoot at tame-ish geese that run their footweb races
over top of the water, racket up
in a concatenation of splashing. Fire and fire
through wingbeat, beak,
throat, honk, thrash, thrash
of feather. Shitty kids miss them,
not for lack of trying. *She's ugly, damn!*

℥

...*damn!* I hear across water. I look.
One, two, half a dozen little guns aim at me.
Close. Fifteen, twenty feet maybe, away. My lungs,
my blood pound pound pound rushing hits the top of my head,

the pop song roars and jerks
PISSING THE PISSING THE PISSING THE NIGHT
I breathe
faster as the morning's slow hard
pink and gold geesey breathing's driven down
to six empty dark holes pointing at me.

☙

I think I breathe, I think I don't,
I think I can't, I think I raise my arms up
over my head like "don't shoot."
I think the kids don't know what to do,
and I think that's bad. I think the snow geese
settle to the water. Their feet coming down
sound on the surface like water
shooting from a Supersoaker, their necks
hooked like triggers, heads like mallets.
Bang bang, kids say, *don't move, you're dead.*

☙

I laugh,
two bullets answer
aimed deliberately five yards away
purple loosestrife splatters

☙

And I pee a little in my pants standing
before
the guns of my grandmother's best friends' great grandkids
which pisses me off, pisses me more off,
which breaks the fear. I turn. I mean

I turn my arms around and—*pissing the night away*—
give them the finger with both, both my hands.

It's something or dumb luck, they giggle,
lower their guns,
fall down almost
with their bodies' jerking.
Flap their arms like wings.
Dumb bitch pussy they scream to save face.
They mean I'm one of them.
Fuck you! My words back to accept.

Crotch wet.

Accept it scares the geese back up.
Accept that like terrified dumb lucky geese
we're all of us new, and scared, and rising.

Fishtown Song

We turn with the river, our streets
don't match up with other city streets.
North may be west, south may be east.

Did I tell you about the tracks, the old coal cars
that stood? My mother had me the night
she sat out under awnings, hearing sounds in the night.

Most of the men put on helmets, went off to fight
the war. At home missing them was another fight.
They had kissed our mothers behind standing coal cars.

And when in the churches there began singing,
and when the stars seemed also singing,
coal cars, the winds through done factories, singing,
our lonely mothers went on singing.

Romance Novel

Smoky cold air came in when he opened
the door. He's brighter than the world behind
him, certainly more solid. There's hello
and damn you all in his smile for the room

and he makes for me and I am his straight
away, in the first few glimpses. I dreamt
I had many gowns, that this hard hard hand
ripped them off, one after the other. Green

one, rip. Blue, *zap*. Yellow with red flowers,
gauze insets. *Kazut, ffffrrrrrrrrrttt*. We reached the zig-
zag, came to the honeydew—

The industrial laundry's heady bleach
dizz seeped into the gray gold street I
walked on alone. As if a bird formed it-
self out of my breastbone and flew off. As

if I walked through stands of blasted cedars
shaking down sapped drops of leftover rain
from prehistoric crooks and limb lops—

Breast. Mouth. Thigh. Zipper. Cream.
Repeat.
Breast. Mouth. Thigh. Zipper. Cream.

Make babies. Here come the babies. The End.

Bulrush

Every damned day I think of my child,
little floating accidental, couple

cells, couple pretty pretty curls, I put her in
the many-babies river, I kissed her

off, good go, good go go away
from me and not be mine my

little reaching
little fingery

thing.

Bollocks by the Thames

This is what I saw:

Condoms starring the river path, all the
blow jobs gone home with dawn. Some boys
come walking along this walkway talking of
"Seals?!"—"Well, they say it's the cleanest
metropolitan river"—"But, seals??!!" and away
beside the slightly jolting green gray river
and then just one drunk woman left
bulling around in the flower beds, slopping
her beer all over the irises, coughing, calling,
contempt-filled, triumphant, to the boneskinny man
struck silent with her and wine, hollow
bottle two-hand clutched, tapping the bench
with it, his throat torqued out like a heron's, sometimes

shh-shhshing her, wincing. A cop-type coming
out of the back there from the shed, peaked
hat, hands not swinging, held out
inches from his uniformed hips, him clearly
firm about her getting out of there,
her shouting "fucker" and "wanker" and "bollocks"
and still him firmly waiting and her head shaking
doggishly as if to shudder off her face-flesh.
Beer on the flowers, down her shirt, slapping
up out of the can-hole, cop-guy pushing her
from the garden though never laying on
his hands. They're like two repelling
magnets, her backing from his push,

shocked, stunned, electrically separate,
her halting her bigness over his small

self, her screaming. "Yeh only 'ave
one loife. Enjoy it!" Her wino boyfriend
skinking off after her between some
trees. "Bollocks!" Her call coming back
into the garden. And the cop-type coming
over, sheepish, laughing that his mother
said "bollocks" all the time: "'all
bolloxed up' she said," he said, "and no
idea it meant testicles," rolling that last
off his tongue like a chitter of curly birds,
blushing: "Shite, sorry, I don't even know you."

That's what he said to me.

Ice

A mother takes her daughter over it, mother in rented brown skates,
daughter in stiff booties that don't bend when her ankles
try to collapse. The mother holds her daughter up
by sheer force of muscle till her arms get tired.

The father is busily driving somewhere,
in a boxy red car or a long blue station wagon.
He hits ice. The mother
grabs the door handle using those same muscles.
The daughter sleeping in back wakes up into the spin.

Signs, poles, wires, trees, passing cars
merge to striated blurs.

The thin covering of snow on the grass off the edge of the road
will have a snow-angel of car tracks after they stop spinning.

Water

The mother shouts at the lifeguard,
shouts, the daughter can see.
The daughter sits on the grass in the field
outside the pool. Link fence. Gnats hang

in shimmers. The daughter 15 now,
ready for something,
not sex. Bare legs. Watches the lifeguard.
Water rocks in the cool shut blue pool.

That was thunder, says the lifeguard.
Just a truck, hitting a bump in the highway,
shouts the mother. *This pool*
should be open! My daughter's
on swim team. She can't miss her workout!

The lifeguard gets up. Bends and pulls
lane lines from the water, red linked beads,
winds them to dripping coils on the deck.
Bitch, the daughter sees him say

with his lips as he works and walks
away from his chair and the mother still standing.
Mother's muscles wrapped around her bones.
Old bitch, he says to the daughter, passing.

My mother, says the daughter, sudden, soft.
Her water rises. Rises with her blush.
Ready for something. He turns, stares,
sorry. But you're right, she says.
Guilty. Hoping rain will come.

Steam

City winter night the mother
walks with the daughter. We see
steam wavering, churning
from manholes. City boiling
itself underneath.

We throw our two shadows
on the shining steam plumes;
it makes tunnels, body-shaped,
into thick steam, a way to
see through to the other
side. I think

my mother is turning to steam.
Thinning. The muscles
going off the bones. Daughter
boiling off the mother.

Moving Her Around

He leaned her up against the wide store window. He took his tattooed
arms—there was a serpent, there a turtle, there some faded

garlands, webs and banners, and also there, pajama'd Max,
jumped off the pages of *Where the Wild Things Are* to war-dance over

the muscles of his forearm—and put them by her, and took them
     back,
and took the bottom of her white shirt and rolled it up her belly,

brown and flat as a shined wood box, and she laughed and laughed
     and laughed.
Later she sat into the boat of his body on the low stoop,

she put her hand on her thigh, he picked it up again
and together they looked at the small red rose scratched there.

And moved it, he did, her hand, back over the rose, but pursed
it first to palm a cup of air, and its stem

stuck out in the shape of a thorn. Later, when he picked her up
and sat her down on his Honda, it lowered its backside with

the weight of her climbing around. Sometimes these boys and girls
are monstrous as goslings tilting on big feet before their feathers grow.

Sometimes they choose an early perfection, or come into it shocked
     and delighted
as a virtuous inheritor. Later, walking with her mother, both of them

boyless against a gray wall of future, she said amazed,
"I just thought he was attractive whatever, I was just talking to him

whatever, and then—" and this song moved their footsteps together:
Oh you go behind me, before me, around me. How is it you go so behind me?

The Kites

Cat boats wait down by the water, rig
tackata-tacking. Kites knotted to masts lash
above: a diamond, a dragon, a booming bird,
made of crackling paper plastic, details
trailing down, following. This is a habit of this
part of the beach. Sometimes a husband of
this or that woman gestures from overfed
loll at a kite as if to say *that's me, that's*
what I've done, as if he, his achievements,
were tied, tugging and skirling, at the end
of a reel, to something big and material
but about to swim should the ocean
come in that far: what can he do about it?

Trooper

We sat down when snow that hadn't yet turned
to hail was coming down, large pats of it,
coming fast, well-spaced, as if with purpose.
We sat down and stretched our backs to keep

from aching too soon, modeled ourselves
after the sky, taking up tremendous stretches,
filling, if we could, it all in, while
the bully wind battered us about the face

and shoulders. Out came the state police,
in shields, helmets, batons, and jerked us
around. Never clubbing, you couldn't say that,
but El was sore for days, and Sylvia,

she had to get her glasses fixed because
they flew off her nose when they flung her
toward the door. "Seemed like they were picking on
the oldest ones among us," Mary says. "Twice

I found myself in a pile of middle-aged ladies
all arms and legs with El and Syl and
Sister Margaret too. Absurd! And when they
started with Frank, I crawled over to him

on my hands and knees, took his hand
to coach him. I felt one of their shields hit
the back of my head. Then the baton came
around my waist, then they took the time

to move it up around my breasts, make that breast,
I've had a mastectomy, then jerked me back—
I tell you if I hadn't been trained
to relax with the flow of energy of the baton,

I would've been hurt bad. No arrests
today. Just as well. I tell you,
the city cops are better by far. Sometimes
indeed they are quite respectful. When

will these guys learn they'd better throw their lot
with the poor or they're going to be
in a deep load of trouble? I tell you, you
can count on it, these are the last rattlings

of capitalism. I most likely
won't be around to see the change over
but it's coming honey, it is coming.
Now when will this damn weather get better?"

Wit's End

My father says, "Face it, you live
    in a civilization of mirrors and sinks,"
        invading my real room, the bathroom.

I pull down an eyelid till I see the pained
    pink meniscus underneath. I "O"
        my mouth, poke the mascara wand

at my eyelashes, not missing
    by much. It's makeup's premonition
        of sex in the house he can't stand.

The bathroom's littered with eyeliners,
    tweezers, kisslipped tissues. I shed snarls
        of hair in the shower like saffron threads,

red kelp. In the mirror I paint myself a clownface
    copied from *Sassy, Seventeen, Glamour.* He
        stands in the doorway, loving

the used-to-be lovable 12-year-old
    formerly his. We look in the mirror:
        blush welts, orange, riding low

on my cheeks, pink lipstick leaking
    from my lip-corners. Glitter-white
        chevrons for eyelids; Cover Girl fails

again to cover my nose-zits. Reflected, behind me,
    tangles of the unwashed bras I don't need
        trail from shower-rod, shampoo rack,

hot-cold dial, soapdish, stopcock.

      He hates it: me mooning, me sighing,
         me incessantly hairbrushing, singing stupid

love songs. "I'll buy back the gunk!" he says.
      He'll pay twice what I spent if only I'll stop.
      I stand by the tub in the bathroom,

my real room. I prop up a leg, I pull up
      my skirt, start shaving thigh-stubble. I shove
      the door shut between us with my ass.

III

Azalea Garden

Flowers heaped on heaped flowery bush, banks
of candy colors. For photos the maids come,
flamingo dresses, tresses up, toestepping around their brides

so heels don't sink in grass. Birds chip, bugs thrum
in the bending of trees, and the maids in their ranks
smiling, smiling, with the tired brides, the tired brides.

Groundsmen call (backs bent, over open spaces,
leaves, weeds, in fistfuls: hands plunge into sacks)
their workman calls. They're bored by the brides.

Grooms are handgripped through their paces
by congratulating uncles and ushers. Black backs,
white fronts, basically backdrop to maids and brides.

Cars hiss past. Blap blap: shoes of runners.
Tarp shake, rake sound. Fat kids bike thin paths,
stop and gape, at the brides, at the brides

who shake their veils, nest into grooms by birdbaths,
nest into wide maids' azalea dresses. Hothouse summer
flamingo flowers sag. Into the sun squint the photographed brides.

The Means

After the month's best lovemaking
means I wake up to ants trailing

all over the house I know it's spring
means I drink one with my first

glass of water at the sink, means
it buzzes on my tongue then stops. Shocked
and shuddering, I pull it out, flick it
still faintly wiggling down the garbage
disposal, grind it dryly up, then
take out a whole troop with a slosh
of jug water, means—God

am I writing poems about killing ants
now? Well, means my tongue's going to

buzz all day, first there where
the ant struggled, then multiplying
insanely over my tongue's mythical
quarters, you know: sweet, bitter,
sour, then, gaggingly, at throat's back,
salty. Means still at the sink, I menstruate

suddenly and urgently, which explains
the morning's woozy ache. Means later, kill

an ant pit-patting up my kitchen
door. I spared it on its way
down, but should it be allowed
to press its luck if I'm not?

Nervous Soprano:	Here are bows for making last year's blouse new;
	tacky rickrack, satin roses, tiny beads, fishline
	to string them all through party hairdos. Here are
	fabrics, velvety couch covers, batiked or swirly,
	that make nude skin feel good. I touch them.
	"Never mind," I think. "Fuck this dress anyway."
Chorale:	Seaflowers on a deepsea background. Swimming,
	slightly shimmering.
Countertenor Sympatico:	"I need new buttons for a sea-blue dress," she tells me.
	She takes it scrunched, crushed, out of her knapsack.
Soprano:	"My lover who left gave it to me," I say to the clerk.
	"He said he got it before he knew we were breaking
	up—
	why didn't I just take it—I did—immediately snipped
	off
	the buttons in fury—threw them away—but stopped
	there."
Chorale:	Seaflowers on a deepsea background. Swimming,
	slightly shimmering.
	Bow in the back, scalloped sweet neck. The sleeves are
	foamy caps.
Soprano:	"Men suck," he says.
Countertenor:	I take the dress, shake it out.

Soprano: Along the store's longest wall, on shelves, cardboard
boxes of buttons rise. He pulls down boxes, opens the
tops.

Countertenor: Soft, she says "I never had a dress like this."

Soprano: He shoves searching fingers through buttons
organized by color, shape, sheen and size.
I put on the dress—it opens all the way down the
front—

Countertenor: over her chinos, her tee-shirt with the holes in it.
It falls around her pants legs, flaps a little;
she holds the empty buttonholes shut.

Soprano: "This dress is you," the little clerk says. And
"it isn't your past, it's your future."
I dance it a little, spinning it around.

Chorale: Seaflowers on a deepsea background. Swimming,
slightly shimmering.
Bow in the back, scalloped sweet neck. The sleeves are
foamy caps.
How it flares, how it goes with her skin.

Soprano: I don't notice him slowing down.
I don't see he's almost crying,

Countertenor: buttons like pirate treasure heaped around me,

Soprano: all the rainbow pirate colors,
also all the anti-rainbow pirate colors,
till he takes the dress off my shoulders,

sits on a stool by the cutting table,
lays it empty over his lap.

Countertenor: I pat it where the buttons
and her breasts would be.

Soprano: "Men suck, they do," he says,
and it's then I see in his eyes,
it's myself in his eyes,
his sea green eyes.

(Repeat from "I don't notice him . . . ," especially the lines "all the rainbow pirate colors," "Men suck, they do," and "it's myself in his eyes," as she takes the dress, walks a last walk around A Button Store.)

Chor., w/Sopr. & Ctrtr.: There are no buttons
There are no buttons
There are no buttons for this dress.

(Brushing a few fripperies with her hip, her thighs, she exits. Her sea-dress fills her hands.)

Only Envy

Some kids scoop handfuls of exploding caps out of big denim pockets,
hurl them down by ones and threes, ratatat;
boys lean against a green wall eating pizza shiny with grease;
my shadow over the face of a sleeping flatnosed drunk,
my shadow over the snob boy drawing him badly,
sex going on all over the place,
the rankness of garbage and
the bimbo of the world. Not jealousy, not lust.

                                          Only envy,
which walks streets at their most crowded hours,
stales and sours like milk in the brain,
like virgins who stay virgin past health and all believing.

One in the Hand

They fight across the lawn away from the sconces
and party lanterns. They fight to the feathery far edges
where the light grays out. Another idiot-nothing fight—

You Always! You Never!—nobody hopefully
to hear. Around behind the curved row of bushes,
dark as nests, "I got to piss," he says, takes his cock out.

He turns his head to watch for watchers, like the man
in the Flemish genre painting who unsheepishly pees
against the wall in the peasant wedding scene. She's

arguing watching his arcing stream, little lights
sparking in it. They fight. It's all that shines. They stop.
Another time and place, Constantin Brancusi,

1926, brings Bird in Flight to America. One look
and the customs official says it isn't art, maybe
a propeller, some kind of a paddle, classifies it

"miscellaneous utensil," levies a tariff. To the judge
at the appeal who asks with a real look of interest on his face,
"What makes you call it a bird?"—"I feel it is a bird."

When he's done, shaking, she roars back, keeps on,
on, on at him. Here it usually escalates or sulkily stops.
He turns, "Hon," sort of laughing, but mad,

pissed, you could say, cock hanging out, full frontal,
"Can't I even piss in peace?" Across the yard
wedding guests' utensils clink glassware to make

the happy couple kiss. Here in hedge, just inside
shadow's swerve, can't they change the end? No.
Yes. She stops him zipping. She reaches—"I *feel* it's . . ."

—gives her hand. Feathers. Claws.

Him Again

Where are you? I thought you said
you would be here tonight. I thought
I was feeling better, maybe not. Sorry, I just
want to tell you—was that a beep? I think
your machine isn't recording any more. Well
last night my mother called, asked
what you mean to me. "Nothing, ma," I said.

Wanted to know "is he serious." "Am I, ma,"
I said, "the question is" (I lied). I should go
but last night I woke up to shouting. A man:
"Leave me alone, you bitch!" I looked out, I saw
only a woman, rain touching her bare shoulders,
sobbing, "wait, wait, please wait," standing
in the rain, then running.

Princess Counting Peas

This springtime of eggs finishing tick, tick, tick,
out of my body.

Here is one for each of my lovers,
here is one for tonight's hanging planet,
one for the best man I let go.
None for the future.

Now I will take a cot and put it by windows,
take the sum of my many years' months' blood,
wait on my thin mattress for the hard knowing to come
of what I have got and done.

The Bombing of Serbia

I. The Beauty of Boys on Skateboards

For they have clean necks, these boys on skateboards.
Their clothes furl about them, shaken by
wind across their shoulder blades, their jeans
hung by nothing over bony hips. One, two,
three, four, five, they pass, *kshoong, kshoong,*
in even beat, all but the last, who pushes
harder to stay in line. Each beautiful
as the others, even this last, he too
more beautiful than anything else—
this street, that sky, cut to battlements by
these buildings—and they are proud, unhumbled,
so long as they shove and roll. I think
they are somewhat like seahorses, curled
in opposite directions, head and tail, top
and bottom, with other humps between.
They bow their heads, feel the rush and hum
across their cheeks and noses. Their hair
whaps, jets; each gathers one knee up—
corrupted soldier's march form—then thrums
foot to ground and shoves. From backs
or chests made of rock or music or rock music,
their arms switch or hang, in haughty nonchalance.
Legs kick, feet flick, heads rear. To soften,
to extend these moves, they hang all this
on the dusk a bolted beat. Then heads turn
down again, knee returns . . . swift! street's barren!
they're gone, dazzling, swum short-sleeved out
on the laughing, crying tide of April spring.

II. River

Rain had our city river coughing up brown
from its impacted bottom. From the bridge
it looked terrible. From the bank it slid
like a stageful of violins. Here is where the boys
fell down under water, slid down, couldn't
get back up. Even dying, maybe the river slime
seemed grotesque, maybe they feared
to touch their naked feet to bottom. Or maybe
it was a great black thrash. Who knows
what colors there are for the drowning.
Their bikes seemed normal, abandoned
on the bank. They left their clothes in sloppy
piles, as if they were from another time,
when one could, as in books, go down a lane
through some woods or a field, jump in a hole
of brown water. Leave clothes on the bank,
fling naked through private air, boy-pricks
twittering, fearful only of a landowner
who'd shoot them. Here is where the sign says
DANGER. It didn't say "rockshelf." It didn't
say "hard current." It didn't say the way
a rescue diver searches for a lost thing
in dark water: dives down, up-out, back, back
down, finally swims to the bank, arms full of boy.

Clean

In a museum, photos:
people later slaughtered stare at a camera.
Ones who are defiant. Ones who are
terrified. Ones young enough to understand

they keep us living petting
our baby chick hearts
a little more tenderly. The latest useless

sorrow. Our helpless selfishness. Let
the world go sadder. And clean.

Strike

I.

When the buses stop running, the union treasurer
walks on bare summer legs, in pink, swell
pink heels, smiling, to the gate where her pal
the union prez will come. The press walks
him in, orbiting him with their hard TV
lights, mikes like fists in his face. They stop;
he keeps walking, like one throwing off
a robe he doesn't care for any longer,
into the mass of rallying rank and file;
they smack his back, grip his hands, part
like the ocean for Moses; when he reaches her
and the rest of the gang, he stands at the gate
dead center of the packed horseshoe of seats
at city council chamber's edge. She pats his shoulder
when he refuses to sit, eyes bugging out, listening
to council resolve nothing. Rank and file
surge a little then, excited by their anger
to more anger; their chanting fills the room
like steel, like polished hardware, *no contract, no work,*
no contract, no work. It rings the roof. The boy
reporter wanders the room (assignment:
get quotes from the guys. You know, do they
really support all that grandstanding? wouldn't they
rather go back to work?). A union driver
fixes him with a voice clear because quiet
under the chanting, explains, hands lain
against his tee-shirt's union logo, *forty-seven*
givebacks, okay, and most illegal, and when

the reporter interrupts *but what about,*
but what about, others join the man patiently
explaining. Their words sucked under. The city walks.

When the El stops rattling over tracks,
and the subway sends no more hot stink and whoosh
through pavement grates, TV catches the scene.
Scores walk at the camera, pass to the side.
Some stop to comment, principally bad-tempered ones
who scowl, finger the air, aggrieved. *Fire them all,
hire students!* (cut) *Welfare moms to drive those trains!*
that'd show them a little something (cut)
Sanguine types swing their arms, commiserate,
flying new on deep-muscle euphoria. *Woo!*
My feet! Lost three pounds, haven't moved
so much in years! (cut) *I recommend*
a new pair of soft-soled support shoes
(cut) A commentator comes on, recites
his self-pleased woe all over again. *As malaise*
sets in (cut) Summer storms bring trees down
across major roadways, screw things up
the worse (cut) *Really you have to want*
to laugh a little. Quiet in the streets.

III.

The men and women—managers, board members—
who run the Transit Co. ride elevators
as usual to their offices. Senior newscasters
with high-rank hairdos and high-salary suits
follow them into featureless boardrooms where
they swing their arms in for crashing corporate
handbone handshakes, laugh nervously as if at jokes
not quite funny. The Vice President for Communications
gazes through rimless glasses to just over where
the camera's eye seeks his. *What we'd*
really like to know is do rank and file
really support all that grandstanding? Wouldn't they
rather go back to work? The managers all shift
a little then, as if to try to seal off
their remaining chinks and penetralia.

Regional rail from the suburbs runs all through
the strike. Different contract. Different deal.
TV shows trains shoving along trash-treed tracks,
trains that slow, slide on wet leaves, lose power,
blink, rebegin; the commuters groan at each delay,
go back to reading, a woman her mystery novel,
another her financial page, a man, sports scores;
a girl, 14, closes up her Entertainment Weekly,
writes in her journal. A woman in the seat
behind her strains to see—throat hurts
from too many cigs, ass hurts from
fucking up against the house all night—
and as they pass packs of empress trees,
rose of sharon, mimosa, ailanthus, she thinks
with the rhythm of the train of the sprinkler switching
switch, switch, swatch, switch, over the grass
at her old small-town house back home. It's a comfort
in this day and computerized age that on,
say, the R3, that goes southwest out of town,
conductors still stagger live down the aisle shouting
names of stops—49th Street, Angora, Lansdowne,
Gladstone, Primos, Secane, Morton, Swarthmore—
unlike on city buses, where drivers in normal times
set going the computer lady's stay-calm voice
telling you where to get off, what to change to.

During the strike some of the drivers
deliver pizzas, some drive the casino buses, trucks.
Izzie coming home from her overnight at the hospital
thinks of her husband somewhere, wherever, some
motel, probably just now rolling over, grunting,
settling his stubble cheek back into some
stinky polyester pillowcase before he
has to get back behind the truck wheel,
hired for the strike's duration to haul produce—
non-union truck company, how's that
for irony, Izzie thinks—short runs, one day,
two, an overnight if he goes to Columbus for soybeans,
some days off to take his turn on the picket
line, blocking regional rail till the commuters
go red in the face with fury on TV,
on TV picketing, down City Hall.

City Council advises management it better
not run those trains themselves. July 4,
people get downtown anyhow, to the grass
overlooking the highway overlooking the river,
three-for-five-buck glowsticks clenched
in wibbly-wobbly sheaves in vendors' fists;
cross-legged, watchers hand up dollars and coin.
Soon pink-green-violet sticks collar
so many necks that in deepening dark it's all
you see, that candy shine, plus hissing sparklers
lighting light-clouds on that field. A lighted
boat parade processes by, wheeling lights,
blinking corporate logos, fireboats spouting up
dirty water in dye-reddened streams,
and a hundred girls clothed in glitter whirl
100 white-silver hankies on a tourist boat deck.
The fireworks are better than ever before,
all intersecting tassels, swift smokes and bursts,
though one guy wants to know where those keening
sperm-bee looking ones of his youth
are gone. His wife, a Transit Co. token seller,
shrugs, pleased at their common remembrance. From when
they were still separate but heading towards
each other. Puts cheek to his shoulder.
Through the finale, the crowd flees to beat the crowd.

VII.

The morning after, discarded glowsticks striate
the grass, pushing leftover weak shine into morning's
full force. Other municipal unions threaten solidarity
strikes, vow to be jailed before giving in.
A food bank's set up for strikers' families.

40 *Days,* 40 *Nights* cry the headlines
one day. Momentarily, with that biblical
alarum, things cheer up, blood runs faster,
new jokes are told, the weather holds a mild
course, catbirds and grackles plaster the parks
with their gabbling noises. Workers go to bars
to talk; TV cams follow them in. *Get your*
boots out. We're going to work tomorrow,
I guarantee you. Meantime a mother paints black
around her eyes to go to court, they look like
little hard nuts. Her bangs divided and glued
in a dozen little strips. She (white) acted lookout,
then danced when the men (white) flooded
the house across to keep the mother (black)
from moving in, danced in the street and high-fived them.
Dumb shits, says an old neighbor. *If they were smart*
they'd pour shellac down the chimney, it would
seep into the bricks, fill the house with poison smoke
if anyone turned on the heat. They'd do it in
the middle of the night and then they'd keep
their dumbshit mouths shut. The mother (black)
saw what they'd done, thought *who needs this shit,*
went back down the steps, which tilted anyhow.
Give me decency, the mother (black) thought,
and her mind took up from there, righteous, outraged,
bored. The mother (white) was thinking property
values, she wanted to make it into the next day,
not have to know anything more than she
already knew; and she lied about it. She gets
five years for that. Her heartbroken children
sob. Friends (black) testify on her behalf: *she's*

no *racist*. She says she didn't mean it; her husband
says their family's X (fill in ethnic group
here) and proud, doesn't stop to think,
none of us do, what it is they're proud of.

During the strike, here are some other things
that happen: Books read. Weddings. Beatings. Movies
watched. Deaths. Breakups. Births. Pounds lost,
gained. Limbs broken. Plenty of sex,
desperado, habitual, enthralled. Illegal
sales. Repairs. Bankruptcies. Stock market per usual
down-up-down. Trees planted. Money lost, gained.
Mostly lost. Laws passed. Children jump in
pools, the ocean. Jellyfish invade the shore
early. Many stings reported, nothing
serious. Sunburns, melanomas. Palms read.
Hometown baseball losing, mostly. Cab drivers
and parking lot attendants work steadily. And
on the kind of summer night when the heat's trapped
under the sky, and the rowhouses swim in it
like racks of fins, and with your ears in your house
you can track kids driving the streets in their chariots
of thump and shout, with your nose track them by the creepy
smell of pot, it's finished. Some men shake hands.

To entice back angry riders, the Co.
offers free rides; every evening for a week
whole families wait to travel to the other end
of the city, flowing amongst parked cars at bus stops
like the stone soldiers of Qin Shihuang's tomb
where Clinton photo-opped on his big '98
China junket, only blobbier, grabassing around.
Welcome banners flap across turnstiles, and arcs
of balloons, smell of powder and rubber mingling
with the long-unsmelt scent of what comes up
when El-brakes shriek on tracks, taking curves.
Drivers settle into their seats, lean out, wave
in triumph. The new old metallic whoosh of bus,
so long lapsed from the city's repertoire
of sounds, startles at first: you turn and look.
Ditto the subway sound starting behind you,
tearing ahead of you, underfoot, and the first renewed
sewerheat blat washing your already hot
legs in your shorts. In photos the union prez's
face relaxes; the treasurer still reaches up
to pat his shoulder. It's like knit bones.

Acknowledgements

Many thanks to the editors of the following journals which first published some of these poems: *American Poetry Review, Antioch Review, Beloit Poetry Journal, Colorado Review, Cream City Review, Florida Review, Indiana Review, Mudfish, New Millennium Writings, Long Shot, Pemmican, Ploughshares, Poet Lore, Santa Barbara Review, Seattle Review,* and *Threepenny Review.*

I am grateful to the Pew Fellowships in the Arts for providing much-needed financial support during the writing of many of these poems.